Popular Cat Library

Burmese Cat

Justine O'Flynn

Published in association with T.F.H. Publications, Inc.,
the world's largest and most respected publisher of pet literature

Chelsea House Publishers
Philadelphia

CONTENTS

Popular Cat Library

Abyssinian Cat
American Shorthair Cat
Bengal Cat
Birman Cat
Burmese Cat
Exotic Shorthair Cat
Himalayan Cat
Maine Coon Cat
Persian Cat
Ragdoll Cat
Scottish Fold Cat
Siamese Cat

Publisher's Note: All of the photographs in this book have been coated with FOTO-GLAZE® finish, a special lamination that imparts a new dimension of colorful gloss to the photographs.

Reinforced Library Binding & Super-Highest Quality Boards

Library of Congress Cataloging-in-Publication Data

O'Flynn, Justine.
Guide to owning a Burmese cat / by Justine O'Flynn.
p.   cm. — (Popular cat library)
Summary: A guide to the history, feeding, grooming, exhibition, temperament, health, and breeding of Burmese cats.
ISBN 0-7910-5461-6 (hc.)
1. Burmese cat Juvenile literature.   [1. Burmese cat. 2. Cats. 3. Pets.]
I. Title. II. Series.
SF449.B8045   1999
636.8'24—dc21
                                        99-26001
                                          CIP

HISTORY OF THE BURMESE

When cat lovers think of felines of the "foreign" type, the term conveys an image of a very slim cat with a sharply defined triangular face. The Siamese epitomizes this group of breeds. It is the archetypal cat of foreign type. Yet, centuries ago, neither Asia and subsequently the father (or mother) breed for very many present-day breeds, including, in part, the Burmese and its own offshoots.

Indeed, were it not for circumstance, the Burmese would never have had any Siamese in its

In the cat fancy, the overall physical appearance of the Burmese is known as *foreign*, exemplified by a slim body and a sharply defined triangular face.

the Siamese nor the many breeds found in the same region were of this build. It is a type that modern cat show breeders have created, or at least accentuated.

This aspect has importance to the Burmese, which in America today (though less so in Britain) is more reflective of what the Siamese stature originally was. The Burmese, the Siamese, and the Korat all share a very similar ancestry. It was by pure chance that the Siamese was to become the most well-known cat from ancestry. It is a breed unto itself in Asia and has been for at least 650 years. Therefore, we must go way back in time to trace its origins.

WHERE IS BURMA?

Before we look back in time, it is worthwhile for those not too familiar with the geography of Asia to pinpoint exactly where Burma is. Until 1937, Burma was part of India. It is situated to the east of India and became a British Crown Colony until 1948, at which time it gained independence. Its immediate neighbors are China, Laos, Thailand (formerly Siam), and Bangladesh.

It is from Thailand that the earliest records of the Burmese are to be found, which is not to say the breed did not exist in Burma. However, Thailand was invaded by the Burmese during the 18th century. It is possible that the cat that bears the Burmese name was taken from Thailand to Burma by returning soldiers. If this is so, the Burmese is like the Siamese in origin.

THE THAI BOOK OF POEMS

During the period of the Ayudhya (c 1350-1767), a series of 17 illustrated poems was written, which is fortunate for domestic feline historians. The capital of Siam at that time was Ayutthaya, which was destroyed by the Burmese in 1767. Three of the cats mentioned in the poems are well known to us in the West. They are the Vichien Mat (Siamese), the Si-Sawat (Korat), and the Thong Daeng (Copper), which is the Burmese.

These various cats were highly regarded. They were believed to

The Burmese is an intelligent, perceptive breed of cat.

have mystical powers that ranged from controlling the weather to being the means by which human spirits could return to earth. In Thailand, when wealthy nobles, priests, and monarchs died, their favorite cat would be placed into the tomb with them. However, a small hole would enable the cat to leave the tomb. When it did so, it was thought it then contained the spirit of its dead master, which would remain in the cat until the feline died.

This sort of belief, in various forms, is a recurring theme in many cultures, including that of the ancient Egyptians whose veneration of cats is well-documented. The Siamese, Korat, and Copper were largely owned by the royal, the wealthy, and the guardians of the temples.

THE FOREIGN CATS ARRIVE IN EUROPE

The cats of Thailand remained within their homelands until the 19th century. It was during 1871 that Harrison Weir organized a cat show at the Crystal Palace in London; it was a huge success. Among the cats on display were a pair of Siamese that attracted

The Burmese comes in four color varieties, the original of which was sable brown (shown here). The other three colors are champagne, blue, and platinum.

The Burmese is known in the fancy as a mutational breed: its origins trace back to a brown oriental-type female and a male Siamese.

considerable interest. An illustration of them appeared in *The Graphic* shortly after the show. They bore little resemblance to the modern Siamese, looking more like the Burmese, except for the difference in color pattern.

The show marked the beginnings of the modern cat fancy as an organized hobby. Within the next few years, cat clubs came into being, and more and more shows were staged. The new cat fancy quickly spread to America with equal success. It became very fashionable not only to own purebred cats but also to seek out new ones.

Many felines appeared under different names before the cat clubs were able to delineate breed types from true breeds, based on a detailed description of what constitutes a given breed. This was determined by reference to a written standard, the development of pedigrees, and stud books of recorded ancestry.

The term "foreign" was applied to any felines that were thought to come from Asia or other eastern countries. It was noted that some were of a more slender build than the typically robust, stocky cats of European descent. The Siamese became the one breed with whom this term was to be strongly linked. It established a considerable following, a sort of feline dynasty. From this, its color pattern and conformation were transferred by hybridization to create a new generation of breeds.

The importance of this fact denied the Burmese the potential to be recognized many years earlier than was the case. It is known that a Mr. Young of Harrogate, Yorkshire, England imported a Burmese during the 1890s. We know it was a Burmese based on the fact that it was described as "a chocolate variety of royal Siamese cats." It was "a rich chocolate or seal with darker face, ears, and tail; the legs are a shade deeper, which intensifies towards the feet."

At that time, it was regarded as being nothing more than a "sport" — a freak of the Siamese that was unworthy of being propagated. Other all-brown cats were imported from Siam, but no one at the time appreciated that they were a different breed than the Siamese.

Also during the same decade, a Korat was taken to Britain, but at the National Cat Show of 1896, it too was regarded as a poor example of the Siamese and ignored. Given that India, thus Burma, was part of the British Empire, it is entirely probable that a number of Burmese and Korats would find their way to Britain with returning officers.

However, the great love affair with the Siamese meant that breeders and judges were not receptive to the notion that other colored cats from Siam (Thailand) were different types. They were related to the Siamese, but totally distinct, and had been so for centuries. Those who had traveled in Burma and Thailand were aware of this reality, but those

The Burmese is an active cat, but it will be quite content to regularly spend quiet time by itself.

running the show fancy were not. They wanted nothing to do with any other cat from that region other than a Siamese.

During those times, the science of genetics was still in its infancy. Today, we know the Burmese, the Siamese, and the Tonkinese are all individual gene variations in a hierarchical series of pigment mutations known to exist at what is called the full-color locus, or the albino series. The Burmese may in fact be the breed type from which the Siamese developed, so may just be the older of the two, but we will never know for sure.

The situation relating to these three breeds underscores the importance of the chance element in breed development. Had the Burmese and Korat been recognized as breeds in their own right when they were first imported to Britain, the development of the foreign type may have taken a somewhat different path. It's a thought-provoking topic. However, it was not to be, and the cat fancy had to wait for about another 40 years before the Burmese was to be seen again in the West.

Ideally, the Burmese is a cat of medium size with substantial bone structure, good muscular development, and a surprising weight for its size.

THE ORIGINS OF THE MODERN BURMESE

The Burmese breed you see today is not totally original, rather a breeder-created look-alike resulting from hybridization of a true Burmese to Siamese. In 1930, when the Burmese was still an unknown breed in the western world, a US Navy psychiatrist, Dr. Joseph Thompson, returned from Rangoon to America with a pet female Burmese called Wong Mau. With no male Burmese to mate with, the female was paired in 1932 to a fine Siamese called Tai Mau. The kittens were lighter in color than their mother but darker than the Siamese. The males were bred back to the mother, which resulted in some kittens of the dark type, like the Burmese, others of the lighter type. The dark-colored individuals, when paired together, bred true to their color. They followed standard Mendelian laws of genetics. The lighter phase hybrids when paired to each other would again produce both purebreeding dark and non-purebreeding, lighter-colored individuals.

As Wong Mau was from Burma, the breed was named for that country. Following the initial crossings, Dr. Thompson continued with his breeding program with the help of geneticist Billie Gerst. Also involved in those early years was a Dr. Clyde Keeler. Whether or not any other Burmese were imported during the following few years does not appear to have been recorded.

Therefore, it must be assumed that the breed developed from the original gene pool mentioned with the possible addition of further crossings to the Siamese from time to time, though these were always officially frowned upon. Once the color had been established, the Burmese "type" was concentrated on until there remained no trace of the Siamese involvement, which would become totally insignificant with each passing generation.

THE BREED GAINS RECOGNITION

In 1936, the Burmese was given official recognition by the Cat Fanciers' Association (CFA), America's largest cat registry. However, this was withdrawn in 1947 on the grounds of unacceptable breeding practices, such as excessive inbreeding. The situation prevailed until 1957, at which time the breed was once again given recognition and registrations started to climb.

In Britain, the breed remained overlooked until after 1945 when returning soldiers from Burma took pets they had acquired home with them. It is also possible that some cats were imported from

established lines in the USA. The breed was given recognition in 1952 by Britain's ruling cat association, the Governing Council of the Cat Fancy (GCCF).

Although the official standards of the breed in Britain and the US are similar, it is of note that there is a clear difference in the breed depending on what side of the Atlantic you live. In Britain, the Burmese is more foreign in its build than its counterpart in America, where a somewhat more stocky cat displaying a less triangular face is preferred.

The British Burmese is not, however, of modern Siamese type, no more than the American Burmese is of cobby type. They are both variations on the original concept of what a Burmese should look like. This means foreign in the original meaning of the word, not the ultra-thin bodies and exaggerated facial shapes that have become associated with this type name and which represent breeding taken to negative extremes.

A pair of eight-week-old Burmese littermates.

POPULARITY BRINGS PROBLEMS

The Burmese has come a long way from the days of Wong Mau and has established itself as one of the most popular cat breeds in both America and Britain. However, over the years, problems have occurred. In some breeding lines, anatomical defects became evident. To overcome these in recent years, breeders have imported cats from Thailand. This has provided the breed with an infusion of unrelated genes from the original genetic source of the breed. This is sound policy and should insure that the Burmese remains a breed that is not allowed to develop the exaggerations that have become so much a part of some purebred felines.

A BURMESE BY ANOTHER NAME

To conclude this brief review of Burmese history, it is necessary for any potential owner to understand the seemingly complex workings of the cat fancy. The Burmese cat, based on its origins, is dark brown or copper. This begs the question that if a Burmese appears in a color other than brown, is it still a Burmese? This is a common dilemma in many breeds—Persian, Russian Blue, and Siamese.

It is akin to the question of whether a longhaired version of a breed is still a member of that breed. In the cat fancy, the answer to both questions is usually no. Space does not permit discussion on the pros and cons of the subject, but as it has

The Burmese has continued to grow in popularity as more and more people become acquainted with the breed's many wonderful qualities.

bearing on the Burmese, we will end this chapter by reviewing the consequence of such a reality.

In Britain, a Burmese is still just that if it is tortoiseshell in brown, chocolate, blue, or lilac. It may also be a red or cream color, as well as the traditional chocolate and brown with the dilution colors of blue or lilac. If it is any other color or pattern than these, it is classified as being of the Asian group — cats of Burmese type but not of Burmese colors. An all-black Burmese is called a Bombay. A semi-longhaired Burmese is a Tiffany, while a Burmese with a shaded or tipped coat becomes a Burmilla. Smoke-color shades and the tabbies become Asian Smoke or Asian Tabby.

In the USA, things are more complex because there are a number of cat registries, each having its own policy in respect to what is and is not acceptable as a given breed. The breeds already mentioned for Britain, some of

Members of this breed are very intelligent, which is evidenced in many facets of their personality.

which were developed in America, are accepted by some associations but not by others. Additionally, the breed created from Siamese/ Burmese crossings (as in the early days of the Burmese development) has progressed to be called the Tonkinese. Light brown Burmese are known as the Copper in one association.

Each of these breeds has its own standard and is now developing quite independent of the Burmese. This complex situation means that if you live in Britain and purchase a Burmese, it may change breed name if you move to America, depending on its color. If you live in America and change the cat registry you support, your Burmese might become another breed!

It sounds crazy, but it really is a problem because there are valid reasons on either side of the equation for and against the alternatives. However, one thing that will never change is that a sable or seal Burmese will be a Burmese in any country and any association as long as there is a Burmese breed.

Further, if a breed is developed from the Burmese and retains its looks and affectionate nature, it remains a Burmese in its spirit, if not in its name. Through many centuries, this fine feline has retained its looks and character so much that it, rather than the Siamese, is now the choice of breeders when they wish to create new breeds based on solid temperament and good stature.

CHARACTER OF THE BURMESE

A cat is a cat, so the character of one is much like that of another? That is like saying a dog is a dog, or a car is a car, implying that all dogs and all cars are much the same as each other. Cat breeds display differences not only in their physical appearances but also in their characters. Of course, all cats share certain traits, but only a non-cat owner would suggest that all feline breeds are the same under the skin.

The Persian is as different from the Siamese as a gundog is different from a guarding dog breed. Cats can be broadly divided into major character groups just as dogs can. There are the stoic cats of Europe, the more regal Persian and Angora types, and then there are the foreigns. This is a name applied to a type, rather than meaning cats from another country, though this was originally the source of the name. The Burmese is a foreign breed in both meanings.

Burmese are affectionate and attentive. If you want a cat that likes to interact with its human family, the Burmese may be the breed for you.

A SOCIAL CAT

Burmese love people; they hate to be alone and are best suited to homes where someone is generally around to interact with them. When you are sitting down, a Burmese will quickly be on your lap. When you go to bed you can bet your Burmese will beat you to the bedroom so that it can get the best sleeping spot — that's if it decides not to wrap itself contentedly around your head!

Burmese just love to be with their owners so much, it must be said that they can sometimes become a nuisance. Only be a companion to one if you really do want a people cat. They will help you with your gardening, with sorting out the cupboard, and with checking out your groceries when you return from the store.

AN INTELLIGENT BREED

All foreign cats are renowned for their intelligence, and the Burmese is certainly smart. This is not, unfortunately, all good news. Intelligence creates curiosity and observation. A Burmese will observe that you open a drawer or cupboard by pulling on it. It quickly learns how to do this for itself. If it can be done at all by feline strength of paw, a Burmese will do it. Thereafter, a Burmese will open any cupboard that it thinks may contain something of interest, such as food, articles to drag around the home and play with, or a comfortable place to nap.

Nothing is sacred to a Burmese except itself! Its intelligent curiosity can get it into problems when it works out how to climb up something but does not think ahead to the coming down part.

Unlike most cats of European stock, the Burmese can be taught much more readily and willingly to walk on a lead. Like its main ancestor the Siamese, the Burmese has many dog-like qualities. As a result, its intelligence can easily be applied to learning numerous tricks that appear to entertain humans. The Burmese is a great show-off! It likes to be the center of attention and will do whatever it feels is needed to insure that it is everyone's little darling.

PERPETUAL MOTION

Like all of its foreign cousins, the Burmese is a very active breed. It likes to be doing things when not being stroked or cradled in the arms of its human companions. For example, it likes to rearrange indoor plants or see how fast it can climb up the drapes. At other times, it likes to walk along shelves tapping ornaments to see just how easily they can be knocked to the floor!

From these quaint examples of its activity potential, you will understand that you must love your Burmese more than your

Like other breeds of foreign type, the Burmese is an active cat that needs suitable outlets to expend its energy.

The Burmese has a soft, sweet voice, but it won't hesitate to vocalize loudly when the occasion calls for it.

ornaments or other frivolous objects that it assumes have been placed there for its own amusement. If you are prepared to accept its antics as mischievous, cheeky, or other appropriate adjectives, you will be delighted with a Burmese. It is a cat that loves to enjoy its human companions and life in general.

The best way to reach a satisfactory relationship with this breed and your cherished objects d'art is to keep them somewhere very safe. Also, supply the cat with ample toys and a climbing frame from a pet store to amuse itself with. Not every Burmese is quite the hooligan described here, for even within the breed, each cat is an individual, and some can be very laid-back and demure. However, it would be prudent not to count on this if you are thinking about obtaining one.

A QUIET RAUCOUS CAT

The Burmese has a very soft and sweet voice and this is the one you will most usually hear, but when it does decide to speak loudly, you will become aware that it can do this in no uncertain manner. It is not so much a meow, as it is a haunting yowl of a sound that will quickly have you rushing to find out what's the matter. You probably forgot to leave the door ajar, and the cat is outside, or you have ignored your favorite friend for longer than it wished.

Provide your Burmese with a variety of toys with which it can amuse itself. Pet shops carry a wide array of great playthings for cats.

If its voice fails to gain your attention, it is possible you will suddenly see it hanging from the window. This is a cat that will go to any length to gain your attention and affection.

A HARDY BREED

The Burmese is, in spite of its regal bearing and pedigreed ancestry, a very tough breed in the physical sense. It is not associated with any particular weaknesses in conformation or health. Its short coat also makes it a cat that is easily groomed. A purebred it may be, but this should not be taken to mean it is in any way less able to fend for itself if some street cat happens along and tries to bully it. The Burmese is athletic, intelligent,

and possessed of a very determined nature. It is more than able to defend itself against cats that may even be somewhat larger than itself.

The aggressive side of its nature is normally never displayed to humans. But should a non-cat lover attempt to feign affection, a Burmese will quickly sense this and make it very clear that the attentions of such a person are unwelcome. A Burmese in a bad mood is not a cat one should trifle with.

A KITTEN CAT

If you are the sort who wants a kitten that never grows up, the chances are good you will find the Burmese is just what you're looking for. It matures, of course, yet always retains that kittenish

The charming qualities of its breed are displayed in this three-month old Burmese kitten. Burmese mature more quickly than some other breeds of cat.

Two Burmese engaged in a harmless tussle. If you own two Burmese, they can keep each other company when you are not at home.

innocence and charm. This enables it to go through life causing havoc, yet always be able to rub itself against you as you view the vista of that day's activities and immediately obtain your forgiveness.

When you are sitting quietly after a day's hard work and suddenly hear pots crashing in the kitchen, your Burmese is sure to bring out the best in you as you say, "That darn cat again — I'll kill it!" One thing is for sure: when you own a Burmese, you will be very aware you have a feline friend around the place to make life interesting. This then is the Burmese character. A cat that

somehow always seems to find things to do around the home, yet always finds its way into the hearts of everyone who gets to know it. It will be as happy in a small house as in a palace, as long as its human companions interact with it and give it the affection it craves.

Somehow, if you live with a Burmese and it's not making its presence obvious, you should begin to wonder if it's ill. For all its antics, you would not wish it to be anything other than what it is. Such is the charm of a breed that has turned many "I don't like cats" people into fervent devotees and loving owners.

The color of the sable Burmese is a rich, warm sable brown, with almost imperceptible shading to a slightly lighter hue on the underparts. Otherwise, there should be no shadings, barring, or markings of any kind.

THE BURMESE STANDARD & COLORS

In order to determine the relative quality of a Burmese cat, or any other feline, there must be a standard against which the individual can be compared. The standards are prepared by a panel of experts within each cat registration body. Periodically, these descriptive documents are amended to take account of progress within the breed, or to place more emphasis on a given aspect that may be regressing. The standard can never be precise so is open to interpretation.

Within each standard, points are allocated to various features based on their believed importance within the breed. Any person who has aspirations to exhibit, judge, or breed Burmese should have a knowledge of the standard. Only by constantly referring to it can a mental picture of an outstanding Burmese be developed.

To the beginner, almost any Burmese would seem to be a fine example when he compares it to the standard. The interpretation of the standard only becomes meaningful when combined with the experience of viewing poor, through mediocre, to those adjudged to be outstanding examples of the breed.

A standard gives a "picture in words" of what an ideal specimen of a given breed should look like. The more Burmese you see, the better able you will be to determine what constitutes a good example of the breed.

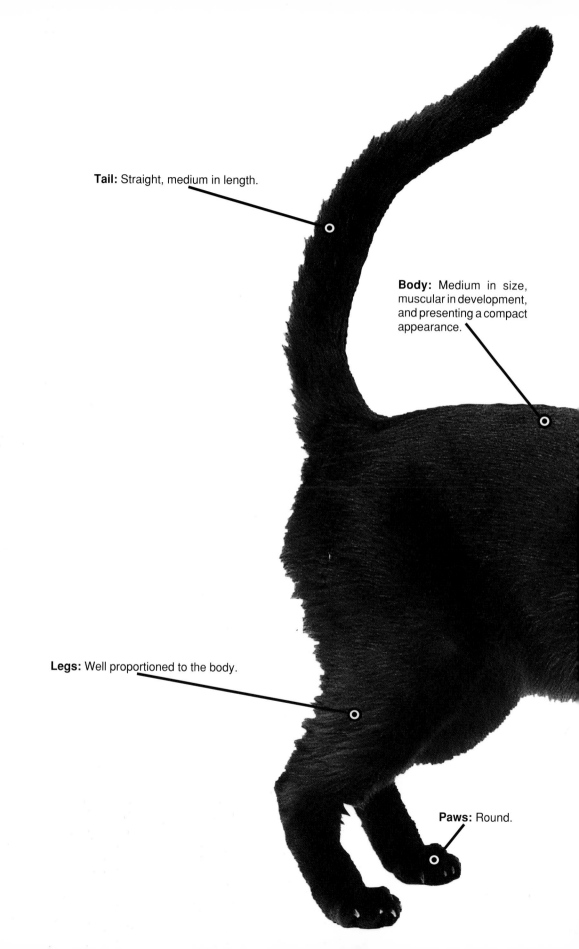

Tail: Straight, medium in length.

Body: Medium in size, muscular in development, and presenting a compact appearance.

Legs: Well proportioned to the body.

Paws: Round.

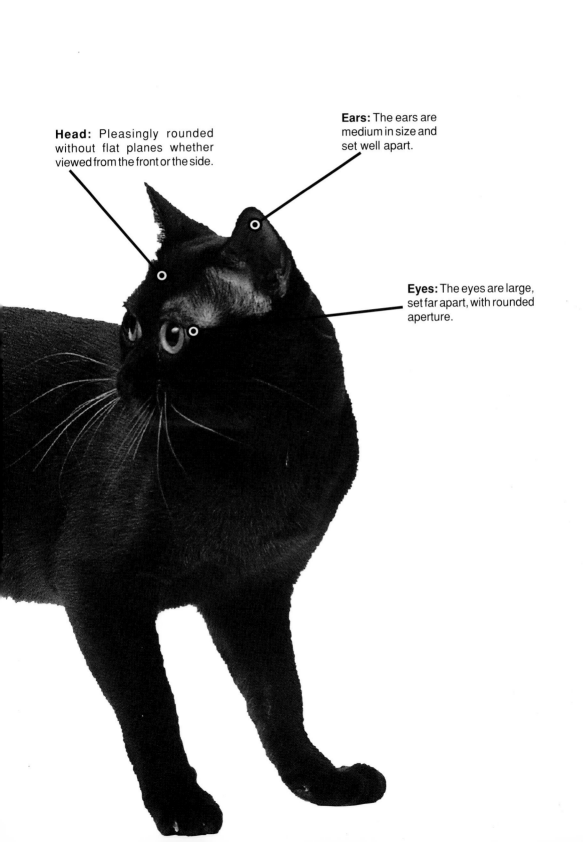

Head: Pleasingly rounded without flat planes whether viewed from the front or the side.

Ears: The ears are medium in size and set well apart.

Eyes: The eyes are large, set far apart, with rounded aperture.

The head sits on a well-developed neck.

THE BURMESE STANDARD

The standard quoted in this text is that of the Cat Fanciers' Association. The CFA is the largest registration organization in the US and the one most Americans will join.

In Great Britain, there are only two registration bodies and of them the Governing Council of the Cat Fancy (GCCF) is easily the most important, and is also the oldest registry in the world.

If you plan to breed Burmese, you are strongly advised to do so only with registered individuals. You should obtain the show standards for the registry that you plan to support.

Point Score of the CFA

HEAD, EARS, AND EYES (30)

Roundness of head 7

Breadth between eyes and full face 6

Proper profile (includes chin) .. 6

Ear set, placement, and size .. 6

Eye placement and shape 5

BODY, LEGS, FEET, and TAIL (30)

Torso 15

Muscle tone 5

Legs and feet.......................... 5

Tail 5

COAT (10)

Short 4

Texture 4

Close lying 2

COLOR (30)

Body color............................ 25

Eye color 5

GENERAL: The overall impression of the ideal Burmese would be a cat of medium size with substantial bone structure, good muscular development, and a surprising weight for its size. This, together with a rounded head, expressive eyes, and a sweet expression, presents a totally distinctive cat that is comparable to no other breed. Perfect physical condition, with excellent muscle tone. There should be no evidence of obesity, paunchiness, weakness, or apathy.

HEAD, EARS, AND EYES: Head pleasingly rounded without flat planes whether viewed from the front or side. The face is full with considerable breadth between the eyes and blends gently into a broad, well-developed short muzzle that maintains the rounded contours of the head. In

The Burmese of today is somewhat heavier than its ancestors and also has a more rounded face.

profile, there is a visible nose break. The chin is firmly rounded, reflecting a proper bite. The head sits on a well-developed neck. The ears are medium in size, set well apart, broad at the base, and rounded at the tips. Tilting slightly forward, the ears contribute to an alert appearance. The eyes are large, set far apart, with rounded aperture.

BODY: Medium in size, muscular in development, and presenting a compact appearance. Allowance to be made for larger size in males. An ample, rounded chest, with back level from shoulder to tail.

LEGS: Well proportioned to body.

PAWS: Round. Toes: five in front and four behind.

TAIL: Straight, medium in length.

COAT: Fine, glossy, satin-like texture; short and very close lying.

PENALIZE: Distinct barring on either the front or rear outer legs. Trace (faint) barring permitted in kittens and young adults. Elongated muzzle with severe narrowing, resulting in a wedge-shaped head that detracts from the rounded contours of the head. Green eyes.

DISQUALIFY: Kinked or abnormal tail, lockets, or spots. Blue eyes. Incorrect nose leather or paw pad color. Malocclusion of

A young female Burmese. Males and females make equally good pets.

the jaw that results in a severe underbite or overbite that visually prohibits the described profile and/or malformation that results in protruding teeth or a wry face or jaw. Distinct barring on the torso.

Burmese Colors

SABLE: The mature specimen is a rich, warm, sable brown; shading almost imperceptibly to a slightly lighter hue on the underparts but otherwise without shadings, barring, or markings of any kind. (Kittens are often lighter in color.) *Nose leather and paw pads*: brown. *Eye color*: ranges from gold to yellow, the greater the depth and brilliance the better.

CHAMPAGNE: The mature specimen should be a warm honey beige, shading to a pale gold tan underside. Slight darkening on ears and face permissible but lesser shading preferred. A slight darkening in older specimens allowed, the emphasis being on eveness of color. *Nose leather*: light warm brown. *Paw pads*: Warm pinkish tan. *Eye color*: ranging from yellow to gold, the greater the depth and brilliance the better.

BLUE: The mature specimen should be a medium blue with warm fawn undertones, shading almost imperceptibly to a slightly lighter hue on the underparts, but otherwise without shadings, barring, or markings of any kind. *Nose leather and paw pads*: Slate gray. *Eye color*: ranging from yellow to gold, the greater the depth and brilliance the better.

PLATINUM: The mature specimen should be a pale silvery gray with pale fawn undertones, shading almost imperceptibly to a slightly lighter hue on the underparts but otherwise without shadings, barring, or markings of any kind. *Nose leather and paw pads*: lavender-pink. *Eye color*: ranging from yellow to gold, the greater the depth and brilliance the better.

Burmese allowable outcross breeds: none.

SELECTING A BURMESE CAT

Burmese come in a range of qualities from the inferior, through the typical examples of the breed, to those which are show winners, or at least potentially so. You may wish to own a high-quality Burmese even though you have no intention to show it. Quality means it will have good bone conformation, the correct stature, and its color or patterns will be of a high standard. Such a cat will be a costly purchase. A typical Burmese will be just that. It will display no glaring faults and its color will be sound. It may display some minor failings in type or color that would preclude it from ever being of show quality.

An inferior Burmese will be one which has obvious faults: either its conformation, its coat quality, poor color or in other ways inferior. Such cats are often described as being pet quality. As long as you appreciate that this term means inferior, its use is fine. However, there are two kinds of inferior Burmese. There is the cat which is inferior only in respect to its type and color—not in relation to its basic structure and health.

There is then the inferior cat produced by those who are in Burmese just to make money. These people have cats that they breed with no consideration for the vigor of the offspring. Such kittens are invariably sickly and prone to illnesses throughout their lives. Poor health and inferior Burmese result from unplanned matings and excessive breeding, coupled with a lack of ongoing selection being applied to future breeding stock.

How do you make the right choice when selecting a Burmese? The answer is you do your homework. Visit shows, talk to established exhibitors, and judges. When you visit the seller take a good look at his stock, and

A kitten should be at least eight weeks old before it goes to its new home. By that age, it will be fully weaned and ready to leave its mother and littermates.

more especially the living conditions of the cats. Is he giving you the hard sell, or does he seem more concerned about the kitten's future home? Sometimes the dedicated seller might even annoy you, but he is concerned for his kittens, even if they are not quality Burmese. The more

The coat of the Burmese is fine, glossy, and satin-like in texture.

Burmese you see, the more likely you are to make a wise choice.

WHICH SEX TO PURCHASE?

From the viewpoint of pet suitability, there really is no difference between a tom (male) and a queen (female). Some people prefer one sex, but this is purely subjective. This author has found males to be more consistent in their character than females, who may tend to be "all or nothing" in their attitude. In other words, they can be extremely affectionate one day, but rather standoffish the next. The tom tends to be much the same from one day to the next, whatever his character might be.

It really is a pot-luck matter just how affectionate a kitten will grow up to become. Cats are very much individuals, and they can change as they grow up. The way they are treated also affects their personality. Therefore, it is more a case of selecting a kitten that appeals to you, regardless of its sex.

Of course, if you wish to become a breeder then the female has to be the better choice. Once she reaches breeding age you can then select a suitable mate for her from the hundreds of quality stud males available to you. If you purchase a male with the view to owning a stud, you are really gambling that he will mature into a fine cat that others would want to use. For this to happen, your tom would need to be very successful in the show ring, and then in the quality of his offspring.

Furthermore, owning a whole tom (a male that has not been neutered) does present more practical problems than owning a queen. Such a male will be continually marking his territory (your furniture) by spraying it with his urine, which is hardly a fragrant scent!

When holding your Burmese—or any other cat—make sure its hindquarters are firmly supported.

If your Burmese is to be a pet only, then regardless of the sex you should have it neutered or spayed. It will be more affectionate to you, will not be wandering off looking for romance, and will not shed its coat as excessively as would an unaltered Burmese. In the case of a tom, he will not come home with pieces of his ears missing as a result of his fights with other entire males. Your queen will not present you with kittens that you do not want but which she will have if she is not spayed. She is far less likely to spray than is the male, but she will show her desire to mate, both with her "calling" sounds, which can be eerie, and her provocative crouching position in which she is clearly inviting a mating.

WHAT AGE TO PURCHASE?

Breeders vary in the age they judge a kitten ready for a new home. An important consideration is obviously if the new owners have experience of cats generally and kittens in particular. While an eight-week-old baby is quite delightful, it is invariably better from a health standpoint that the kitten remains with its mother until it is ten or more weeks of age. Some breeders will not part with a kitten until it is 16 weeks of age.

The kitten should have received at least temporary vaccinations against feline distemper and rabies (if applicable in your country and if the kitten is over 12 weeks of age) and preferably protection against other major feline

Before selecting your Burmese, you should decide whether or not it will be strictly a pet or a show-quality cat.

infections. Additionally, you should let your own vet examine your Burmese.

Although most owners will wish to obtain a kitten, a potential breeder or exhibitor may find that a young adult (over eight to nine months of age) is more suitable to his needs. By this age the quality of the Burmese is becoming more apparent. However, bear in mind that a mature Burmese queen will not be at her peak until she is about two years of age. A tom will be even later in reaching full maturity, and he may not peak until he is five years of age.

ONE OR TWO BURMESE?

Without any doubt, two kittens are always preferred to one. They provide constant company for each other and are a delight to watch as they play. The extra costs involved in their upkeep are unlikely to be a factor if you are able to afford a Burmese in the first place.

Many cat fanciers feel that owning two Burmese is the only way to go and that the extra costs involved in their upkeep are worth all of the enjoyment that they will give you.

Your Burmese can easily keep itself
occupied, but it will greatly enjoy
spending quality playtime with you.

GENERAL CARE & GROOMING

Burmese cats are extremely easy to cater to in terms of their accommodations and general care. This chapter will discuss purchasing the essential and nonessential accessories for your cat, socializing your cat with children and other animals, making a safe environment for your cat, and disciplining your cat the proper and most effective way.

ABSOLUTE ESSENTIALS

While keeping a cat is essentially a simple task, there are certain items that the cat owner absolutely must have if he expects to keep his kitty happy and well. The following items should be purchased from your local pet store or supply center before you bring the cat into your home. Don't try to find bargains! Buy the best the first time and you won't have to replace it as often. Pet shops offer the finest pet supplies, and the proprietors will be happy to advise you which is the most effective and best for your particular cat.

Litter Tray

Every cat will need a litter tray so that it can relieve itself whenever it wishes to. If this is not provided from the outset, the

The Burmese's short, close-lying coat is easy to groom. If you begin a regular grooming program when your cat is a kitten, it will be well acclimated to the procedure by the time it is an adult.

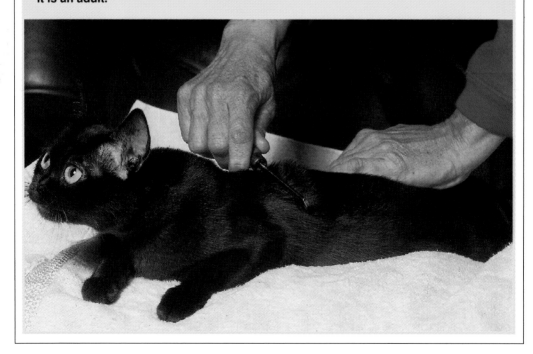

A homemade house provides shelter from the elements for this Burmese.

only possible consequence is that the cat will be forced to foul your carpet or some other surface. There are many styles and sizes of litter trays, and the larger ones are the best for long-term service. Some have igloo-type hoods, both to provide a sense of privacy for the cat and to retain any odors. However, an open tray is just as good and will not in any case be foul smelling if it is cleaned as it should be.

You will need to purchase cat litter for the base of the tray. There are many brands to choose from, and some have odor neutralizers already in them. Cover the base with enough litter to absorb urine and for the cat to scratch around in. In the event you should run out of litter, you can use coarse grade sawdust or wood shavings. These are preferred to garden soil because the latter may contain the eggs of parasitic worms or other parasites.

The tray should be cleaned after each use, removing that which is soiled. A small dustpan is handy for attending to this chore. Once a week, you should disinfect and thoroughly rinse the tray.

The average Burmese litter size is around five kittens.

If you own a cat, a scratching post is a must. This well-designed unit easily accommodates several Burmese.

This Burmese is ready for a catnap. Many cats find that their owner's bed is the best place to sleep.

Housetraining is easily accomplished with a kitten. When you see it searching for somewhere to relieve itself, which will be accompanied by crying, it should be gently lifted and placed into its tray. Never scold a kitten for fouling the floor: it will not understand why you are annoyed with it. You must watch the kitten after it has played and after it wakes up because these are prime times for it to want to relieve itself. Remember, kittens cannot control their bowel movements for more than a few seconds; this time increases considerably as the cat matures. If you exhibit patience, you will find the kitty quickly gets to know what is expected of it. Cats are fastidious about cleanliness, so if they foul the home, there is invariably a

reason for so doing. Often it will be because the litter tray has not been cleaned or you were not around enough when the cat was a kitten.

Scratching Post

Here again, there are many styles to choose from. All have a fabric on them, and the post may be free standing or the sort that is screwed to a wall. You can also purchase carpet-clad climbing frames, which are more expensive but greatly enjoyed by cats. When you see your kitten or cat go to scratch your armchair, lift it up and place it against the scratching post. Gently draw its front feet down the post a few times. Again, if this is repeated a number of times, the kitten will understand that it can claw away

A well-maintained Burmese cattery. These cats have the opportunity to enjoy plenty of sunshine and fresh air.

be able to place a finger between the collar and the cat's neck.

Carry Box

The carry box is so useful that I regard it as an essential item for all cat owners. It will be needed when you visit the vet, when traveling, or when you need to contain the cat for any reason. It also makes a fine bed for a kitten. The box can be made of wicker, wood, wire, or fiberglass. The latter are probably the best but can be expensive if they are of a high quality. It is essential that they should be large enough for the adult cat to stand upright in and not be forced to stoop.

The base of the box can be fitted with a good lining of newspaper on which a blanket is placed. A kitten will find this a nice bed, especially if it has a companion. If not, place a cuddly toy in with it to snuggle up against. When it is a kitten and

on the post but not on the furniture. As it grows older, it will no doubt test your resolve now and then, but usually if you clap your hands and say "No" in a firm voice, it will realize you are keeping an eye on it!

Cat Collar

All cats should wear a cat collar fitted with an ID tag. In many cities, this is a law. An elastic collar wil prevent the possiblility of its getting snagged, thus possibly choking the cat. Be sure it is neither too tight nor too loose. You should

Your cat should be groomed on a regular basis. From brushes to nail clippers, your pet shop will meet your pet's every grooming need. Photo courtesy of Four Paws.

during its first week or so in its new home, it is better that it is confined at night, so it cannot harm itself by wandering about the home. Once it is totally familiar with your home, you can leave the carry-box door open at night so it can come and go as it wishes.

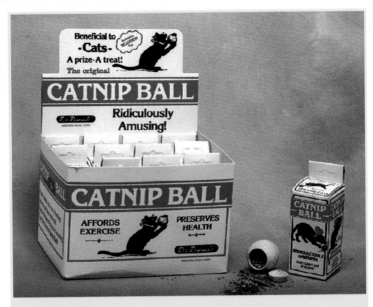

Catnip has long been a feline favorite. Now available in many different forms, this treat will prove to be popular among cats. Photo courtesy of Dr. A.C. Daniels.

Feeding Dishes

You will want one dish for moist cat food, one for dry food, and one for water. You can purchase dishes made of earthenware, aluminum, stainless steel, or plastic. You can also use saucers or any combination of these. The main thing is that they are kept spotlessly clean, so they should be washed after each use. The water dish should be cleaned and replenished each day.

Brush

Cats do not come any simpler to groom than a Burmese. Even so, your cat should have its own brush, preferably of a medium-bristle type. A chamois leather or silk cloth is also useful to give your cat that extra sheen after it has been brushed. Although the Burmese hardly needs any brushing, it is useful to attend to this once a week. This makes your cat familiar with being handled, and at such a time, you can give it a check over. Inspect its ears to see that they are free of wax and check the teeth to see that they are clean. Inspect the pads to ensure that they are firm but supple. Part the toes with your fingers just to make sure they are free of debris. Lodged in the skin, dirt and grass could be the source of an abscess if they are not removed. Gently feel the abdomen to check that there are no swellings.

BEYOND THE BASICS

Pet lovers love to lavish their pet with all kinds of goodies, and for a cat owner, the sky is the limit when it comes to choosing special accessories for his pet. The ever-expanding pet industry makes it easy for cat owners to

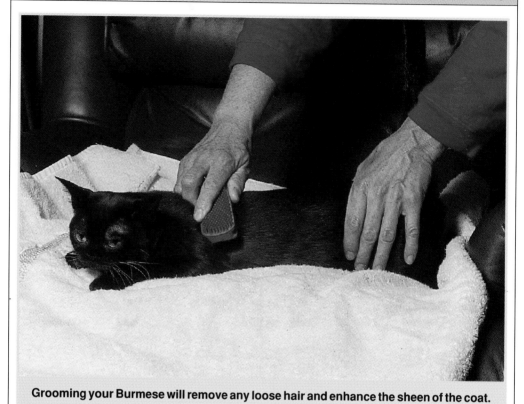

Grooming your Burmese will remove any loose hair and enhance the sheen of the coat.

find new and inventive ways to entertain and better care for their feline friends.

Basket or Bed

If you obtain a carry box for your kitten, then a bed is not a necessity. Cats like to choose their own place to sleep, and indeed they will have numerous places depending on their mood, the ambient temperature, and who happens to be in your home at a given time. Some will have a favorite chair or sofa, some may prefer a secluded spot behind a chair, while others will prefer to sleep on your bed, knowing this to be a warm and popular place with their "human-cat" companions.

Better than a conventional basket would be to invest in one of the many carpet-clad, wooden furniture pieces produced these days for cats. These are fun and take into account the cat's preference for sleeping above floor level. Some cats do sleep in baskets, so it is a case of reviewing all the options and deciding which you think will best meet your needs.

Halter or Harness

If you plan on taking your cat with you on vacation or generally when you travel, it will be found that a cat collar does not offer you full control over your Burmese. Additionally to the collar, you could purchase one of the numerous halters now available for cats. Choose one that fits snugly. Those with top fastenings

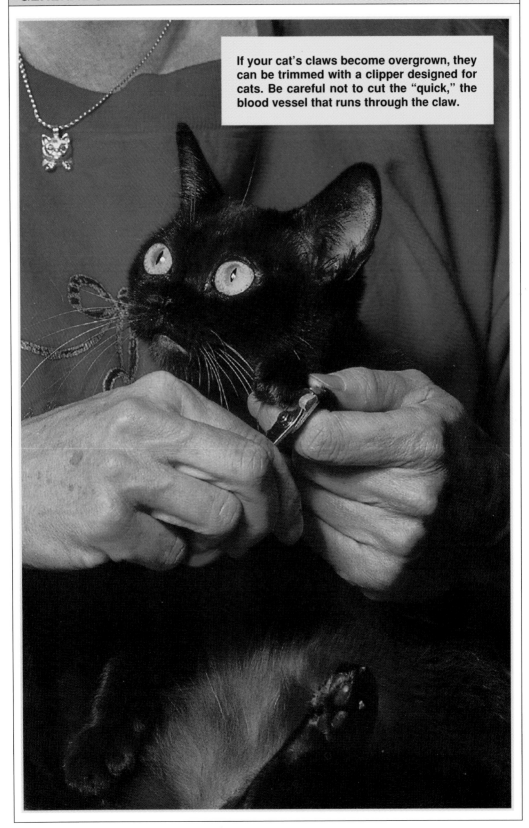

If your cat's claws become overgrown, they can be trimmed with a clipper designed for cats. Be careful not to cut the "quick," the blood vessel that runs through the claw.

Cats love to climb. Your Burmese will no doubt have several favorite spots in which it will spend time.

Do not take the cat from the confines of its home territory until it is really relaxed on a lead. In the event of a dog suddenly appearing, the halter allows you to maintain control of the cat, which should be promptly lifted up. If it is not your intention to take your cat on regular outings, there is little point in lead training it because cats are generally not happy away from their home range.

Toys

There is no shortage of commercially made cat toys these days. Avoid soft, plastic ones that your pet might break apart and swallow pieces from. If you devote time to playing with your cats, you will find that they will learn how to play games with you, and it will strengthen the bond between you and your cat.

The color of these Burmese kittens' coats has yet to be fully developed.

are easy to place on your cat. Do not obtain dog harnesses because they will be too big around the chest, even if they are for small dogs.

Lead training is best done while your pet is young. Place the halter on the kitten and let it become familiar with it before you attempt to attach the lead. When the halter does not bother the cat, you can then attach the lead and let the cat wander about in the privacy of your yard. Here it will become used to the fact that there is a restraint on its movements. The process cannot be hurried because cats do not like to be restricted. Only devote a few minutes per day to lead training and always encourage the cat with a treat.

The face is full, with considerable breadth between the eyes and blends gently into a broad, well-developed short muzzle.

A cat carrier is the best way to transport your cat. This Burmese kitten has been provided with a pillow for added comfort.

CATS AND CHILDREN

If there are young children in your home, it is most important that they are taught from the outset to respect your new kitten or cat. Children must understand that cats should not be disturbed if they are sleeping and should not be handled in an incorrect manner. When being lifted, a cat should never be grasped by the loose fur on its neck. Always support the full body weight with one hand, while securing the cat firmly but gently around the neck with the other hand.

Children should be made aware of the fact that even kittens can inflict a nasty scratch on them if the kitten is not treated with kindness and consideration. Essentially, you must always be watchful if young children are playing with the family cat until they are old enough to understand how it must be handled.

CATS AND OTHER PETS

The cat is a prime predator and should not be left in the company of young rabbits, guinea pigs, hamsters, or mice if these other pets are out of their cage. As a general rule, if a pet is as big as your cat or is another carnivore, it will usually be safe. Cats and dogs get on really well if they are brought up together. However, if a kitten is introduced into a home that has an adult dog, due care must be exercised. The first thing to ensure is that the resident pet gets extra attention so it does not become jealous of the new arrival.

The kitten and other pets must come to terms with each other in their own time and manner — it is not something you can hurry. In some instances, a newly acquired cat may make friends very quickly with dogs or other household cats. In other cases, the best that ever happens is a sort of truce, each accepting the other but avoiding contact most of the time. Kittens will invariably be accepted much more readily than will adult cats. The latter, of course, will have developed their own attitudes to other animals depending on what their experiences have been with them.

SAFEGUARDING A KITTEN

When a kitten is first introduced to your home, there are many potential dangers that it must be protected from. For

Allowing your pet to roam freely outdoors will make it susceptible to a number of dangerous situations.

example, a door left ajar on a windy day could easily slam shut on the kitty. An unprotected balcony is an obvious danger to a young feline, as is a garden pond. An open fire is yet another example of how a kitten might easily become injured. They are, of course, naturally cautious of dangerous situations, but even so, it is best to watch out for them just as their mother would.

The kitchen is probably the most dangerous place for kittens. A typical scenario is that you might turn around from the stove with a pan of boiling water or a kettle in your hand, only to trip over the kitten. The water may

scald the kitten or yourself badly, and the fall would not do you any good either! Kittens just love to pounce and hang onto string and its like. The latter might be the cord from an electric iron you are using — the result being obvious. As your Burmese gets a little older, it will easily be able to jump onto kitchen units and should be educated at an early age not to do this in this particular room.

The other important area of safeguarding a kitten is in relation to ensuring it is given maximum protection against major feline diseases. This is done via vaccinations. Consult your vet about these as soon as you have

It won't be long before this kitten outgrows its bed. When purchasing your cat's accessories, you might want to keep in mind what will adequately meet the cat's needs when it is fully grown.

obtained your Burmese. Do not allow the kitten out of the house until it has complete protection.

DISCIPLINE

Cats are very intelligent and respond to discipline just as dogs and most other comparable pets will. They are not dangerous to people so do not need the level of training that a dog does to fit into a human world. It's really a case in which your cat should understand one simple command—"no." If it goes to scratch the furniture, you should promptly lift it up and say, "No." A very light tap on its rump will enforce the command. This is about the extent of discipline that will ever be needed.

The most important thing you must remember whether training a cat, a dog, a horse, or a large parrot, is that they relate only to the moment. The longer the time lapse between the act and discipline, the less chance there is that the animal will associate one action with another. You can work on the basis that if you are unable to administer discipline within seconds of an unwanted act, you may as well not bother. If the kitten or cat is out of distance, clapping your hands at the same time as saying the command can be effective. Alternatively, you might be able to throw some light object at the cat at the same time as the command is given.

Frequent handling when it is a kitten will help your pet to grow up to be a trusting, affectionate feline companion.

All animal training is based on the fact that the animal associates a given action with a given response. The latter will either be neutral (i.e. nothing happens), positive, or negative. Neither cats nor dogs will understand a lengthy lecture, but they will rapidly understand instant responses to their own actions. You will thus use both positive and negative "enforcers" in training your cat. If your Burmese meows for some food or to go out and you respond promptly, this will enforce the action that will be repeated at a later date. The more you respond, the greater will be implantation of that action in the cat. The same goes for discipline.

You should never need to use forcible discipline with a cat. If you think carefully about any given action and apply an appropriate response fairly and consistently (the latter being crucial), you will develop a real understanding with your feline friend.

The Burmese's head is roundly contoured.
In profile, there is a visible nose break.

FEEDING YOUR BURMESE

Cats and kittens are very much like people when it comes to their eating habits. Some are extremely easy to satisfy; others are much more difficult to please. Adult cats can be a worry, but at least you know they must have eaten something to have survived to maturity. Kittens, on the other hand, can prematurely turn your hair gray because you fear they may not thrive unless you can come up with some delicacy that tempts their palate!

Fortunately, there are so many quality brands of commercial cat foods available today that it should be possible to get even the most fastidious of kittens through its most difficult early months.

CATS ARE CARNIVORES

The cat is a prime predator in its wild habitat, and this means its basic diet must be composed of the flesh of other animals, be they mammals, birds, or fish. The digestive tract of a carnivore has

Burmese are fairly cosmopolitan in their eating habits, and with the variety of commercial foods that are available, you should have no problem providing a good diet.

Treats can be provided on an occasional basis to help provide a little variety in the diet. Some treats act as a cleansing agent to help reduce tartar on the cat's teeth. Photo courtesy of Heinz.

COMMERCIAL FOODS

The range of commercial cat foods encompasses canned, semi-moist, and dry diets. We have always found that our cats have never really enjoyed any of the semi-moist foods. The canned and dry foods come in an extensive range of flavors, which include meat, fish, and poultry. Of the canned foods, some have a firm consistency; others are chunks in a sauce. There are also formulated kitten foods.

Commercial foods can form the basis of your Burmese's diet, but you should supply a variety of them to reduce the chances that some key constituent is missing from the diet. Burmese will no doubt help in this matter because they seem to tire of one brand if it is fed daily. Indeed, deciding which is their chosen flavor of the week can be an interesting guessing game. They will suddenly show no interest in a

A good diet will be reflected in your Burmese's overall appearance.

evolved to cope with proteins, but it has little ability to digest raw vegetable matter. This means the latter must first be boiled, so that the hard cellulose walls of such foods are softened, then broken down by the digestive juices and flora found in the alimentary tract.

In the wild, the cat would eat just about every part of its prey, leaving only the bones that were too large for it to digest. This diet would provide proteins and fats from the body tissues, roughage from the fur or feathers, and carbohydrates and vitamins from the partially digested vegetable matter that would be in the intestines of the prey. Combined with water, a very well-balanced diet would be provided for the cat. An equivalent of such nutrition is what you must strive to supply.

Eye color ranges from yellow to gold, the greater the depth and brilliance, the better.

A kitten will have different nutritional requirements than will an adult cat. If you have any concerns about your Burmese's diet, check with your vet.

foods provide both variety and good exercise for the jaws. Human consumption meats can be of beef, pork, or lamb. All fish should be steamed or boiled, and it is best to stay with white fish such as cod. Tuna, sardines, and other canned fish are appreciated, but only give small quantities of them as a treat because they may prove too rich for your pet's system. Chicken is enjoyed by nearly all cats.

Cheese, egg yolk, spaghetti, and even boiled rice are all items that you can offer to your pets to see if it appeals to them. Small beef and other meat bones that still have some meat on them will be enjoyed and keep a kitten or cat amused for quite some time. Beware of bones that easily splinter, such as those of chicken or rabbit.

product they seemed to eat with relish just a few days earlier! You will find that some cats enjoy fish flavors, others poultry and yet others, the various meats.

Dry food is enjoyed by most, though not all, Burmese. It provides good exercise for the teeth and jaw muscles, which canned foods do not. Their other advantage is that you can leave them out all day without their losing their appeal to your pets, or attracting flies. Water must always be available to your cats; this is even more important if the basic diet is of dried foods.

NON-COMMERCIAL FOODS

Your Burmese will enjoy many of the foods that you eat. These

This mother Burmese watches carefully as her owner checks on the litter. Burmese are said to be good mothers.

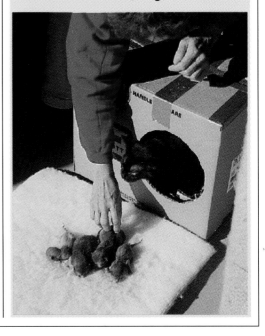

This Burmese is enjoying a treat between meals. Your Burmese will enjoy many of the foods that you eat.

You can by all means see if small pieces of vegetables or fruits are accepted if mixed with the food, but generally cats will leave them. This is no problem providing that the cat is receiving commercial foods as its basic diet. Such products are all fortified with essential vitamins after the cooking process.

HOW MUCH TO FEED?

Cats prefer to eat a little but often, rather than consume one mighty meal a day. However, as carnivores, adults are well able to cope with one large meal a day. The same is not true of kittens, which should receive three or four meals per day. A kitten or a cat will normally only consume that which is needed. You can arrive at this amount by trial and error. If kitty devours its meal and is looking for more, then let it have more. You will quickly be able to judge how much each kitten needs to satisfy itself. Always remove any moist foods that are uneaten after each meal.

At 12 weeks of age the kitten should have four meals a day. One of these meals can be omitted when the kitten is 16 weeks old, but increase the quantity of the other three. You can reduce to two meals a day when the kitten is about nine months of age. From that age, it is best to continue feeding two meals—one in the morning and one in the early evening. How many times a day you feed your adult cat is unimportant. The key

An ideal specimen of a Burmese will exhibit good physical condition and excellent muscle tone.

factor is that it receives as much as it needs over the day, and that the diet is balanced to provide the essential ingredients discussed earlier. It is also better that meals are given regularly. Cats, like humans, are creatures of habit.

WATER

If a cat's diet is essentially of moist foods, it will drink far less than if the diet is basically of dry foods. Many cats do not like faucet (tap) water because they are able to smell and taste the many additives included by your local water board. Chlorine is high on this list. Although it dissipates into the air quite readily, chloromides do not, which is why the cat may ignore the water. During the filtering process at the water station, chemicals are both taken out and added. The resulting mineral balance and taste are often not to a cat's liking. This is why you will see cats drinking from puddles, a flower vase, or even your toilet, because the taste is better for them. If your water is refused, then you can see if your cat prefers mineralized bottled water—not distilled because the latter has no mineral content to it.

Burmese are very inquisitive cats that love to explore their surroundings. You may find that your Burmese will investigate every nook and cranny of your home.

THE NEW ARRIVAL

It is a very traumatic time for a kitten when it leaves its mother and siblings. It will often eat well the first day; however, as it starts to miss its family, it will fret. You can reduce its stress by providing the diet it was receiving from the seller. You can change the diet slowly, if necessary, as it settles down. Of course, many kittens have no problems, but if yours does, this feeding advice should help its period of adjustment.

What is essential is that the kitten takes in sufficient liquids so that it does not start to dehydrate. This, more than anything else, will adversely affect its health very rapidly. If you are at all concerned, do consult your vet. The kitten may have picked up a virus, but if it is treated promptly, this should not be a problem. Your vet might supply you with a dietary supplement, which we have found excellent for kittens experiencing "new home syndrome." After a few weeks, the kittens feel right at home.

A healthy Burmese will be bright eyed, attentive, and alert.

KEEPING YOUR BURMESE HEALTHY

Like any other animal, your Burmese can fall victim to hundreds of diseases and conditions. Most can be prevented by sound husbandry. The majority, should they be recognized in their early stages, can be treated with modern drugs or by surgery. Clearly, preventive techniques are better and less costly than treatments, yet in many instances a cat will become ill because the owner has neglected some basic aspect of general management. In this chapter, we are not so much concerned with cataloging all the diseases your cat could contract, because these are legion, but more concerned with reviewing sound management methods.

HYGIENE

Always apply routine hygiene to all aspects of your pet's management. This alone dramatically reduces the chances of your pet becoming ill because it restricts pathogens (disease-causing organisms) from building

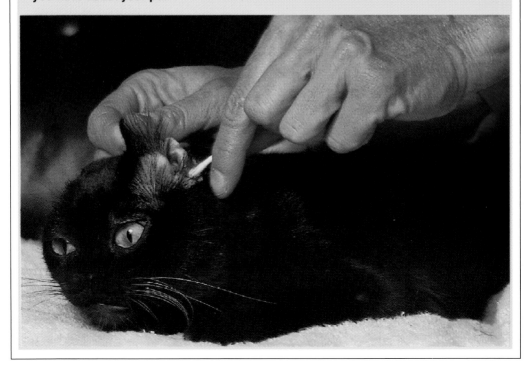

Cats are occasionally subject to ear problems, including ear mite infestation. Treatment for such conditions is fairly simple. Check with your vet about any health concerns that you have about your pet.

up colonies that are able to overcome the natural defense mechanisms of your Burmese.

1. After your cat has eaten its fill of any moist foods, either discard the food or keep it for later by placing it in your refrigerator. Anything left uneaten at the end of the day can be trashed. Always wash the bowl after each meal. Do not feed your pet from any dishes that are chipped, cracked, or, in the case of plastic, those that are badly scratched.

2. Always store food in a dry, cool cupboard or in the refrigerator in the case of fresh foods.

3. For whatever reason, if you have been handling someone else's cats, always wash your hands before handling your own cats.

4. Be rigorous in cleaning your cat's litter box as soon as you see that it has been fouled.

5. Pay particular attention to the grooming of a Burmese cat because so many problems can begin with a seemingly innocuous event. For example, in itself, a minor cut may not be a major problem as long as it is treated with an antiseptic. But if it is left as an open untreated wound, it is an obvious site for bacterial colonization. The bacteria then gain access to the bloodstream, and a major problem ensues that might not even be associated with the initial wound. The same applies to flea or lice bites. Inspect the skin carefully for signs of flea droppings when you groom a Burmese. These appear like minute specks of black dust.

RECOGNIZING AN ILL CAT

You must be able to recognize when your cat is ill in order to seek a solution to the problem. You must learn to distinguish

The more familiar you are with your Burmese's behavior, the better able you will be able to tell when it is not feeling well.

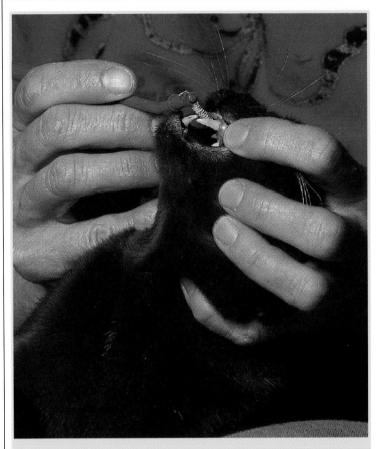

This Burmese is getting its teeth brushed. In recent years, much more attention has been given to cat dental health.

In general, any appearance or behavior that is not normal for your cat would suggest something is responsible for the abnormality. This is your first indication that something may be amiss. The following are a number of signs that indicate a problem:

1. Diarrhea, especially if it is very liquid, foul-smelling or blood-streaked. If blood is seen in the urine, this is also an indication of a problem, as is excessive straining or cries of pain when the cat tries to relieve itself.

2. Discharge from the nose or eyes. Excessive discharge needs veterinary attention.

3. Repeated vomiting. All cats are sick occasionally with indigestion. They will also vomit after eating grass, but repeated vomiting is not normal.

4. Wheezing sounds when breathing, or any other suggestion of breathing difficulties.

5. Excessive scratching. All cats will have a good scratch on a quite regular basis, but excessive

between a purely temporary condition and that which will need some form of veterinary advice and/or treatment. For example, a cat can sprain a muscle by jumping and landing awkwardly. This would normally correct itself over a 36-48 hour period. Your pet may contract a slight chill, or its feces might become loose. Both conditions will normally correct themselves over a day or so. On the other hand, if a condition persists for more than two days, it would be advisable to telephone your vet for advice.

Pet dental products are available for helping to fight plaque, reduce tartar build-up, and control unpleasant breath. Photo courtesy of Four Paws.

scratching indicates a skin problem, especially if it has created sores or lesions.

6. Constant rubbing of the rear end along the ground.

7. Bald patches, lesions, cuts, and swellings on the body, legs, tail, or face.

8. The coat seems to lack bounce or life, and is dull.

9. The cat is listless and lethargic, showing little interest in what is going on around it.

10. The eyes have a glazed look to them, or the haw (nictitating membrane, or third eyelid) is clearly visible.

11. The cat is displaying an unusual lack of interest in its favorite food items.

12. The gums of the teeth seem very red or swollen.

13. Fits or other abnormal signs of behavior.

14. Any obvious pain or distress.

Very often two or more clinical signs will be apparent when a condition is developing. The number of signs increases as the disease or ailment advances to a more sinister stage.

DIAGNOSIS

Correct diagnosis is of the utmost importance before any form of treatment can be administered. Often it will require blood and/or fecal microscopy in order to establish the exact cause of a condition. Many of the signs listed above are common to most diseases, so never attempt home diagnosis and treatment: if you are wrong, your cherished Burmese may pay for your error with its life. Once ill health is suspected, any lost time favors the pathogens and makes treatment both more difficult and more costly.

In making your original decision to purchase a Burmese, or any other cat, you should always have allowed for the cost of veterinary treatment. If this is likely to be a burden that you cannot afford, then do not purchase a cat. The first few months, and especially the first weeks, is the time when most cats will become ill. If they survive this period, the chances are that future visits to the vet will be rare, other than for booster vaccinations.

Kittens do not have the immunity to pathogens that the adult cat does, nor do they have the muscle reserves of the adult. If they are ill, they need veterinary help very quickly if they are to have a good chance of overcoming a disease or major problem.

Having decided that your cat is not well, you should make notes on paper of the signs of the problem, when you first noticed them, and how quickly things have deteriorated. If possible, obtain a fecal and urine sample, then telephone your vet and make an appointment. Ask other cat owners in your area who their vet is. Some vets display a greater liking for cats, or dogs, or horses than do others. This is just human nature, but obviously you want to go to one that has a special affection for felines.

The sooner a health problem is detected, the sooner treatment can be effected. If you suspect that your Burmese is sick, take careful note of the symptoms and contact your vet.

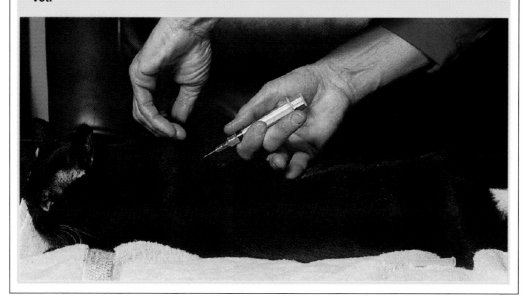

TREATMENT

Once your vet has prescribed a course of treatment, it is important that you follow it exactly as instructed. Do not discontinue the medicine because the cat shows a big improvement. Such an action could prove counterproductive, and the pathogens that had not been killed might develop an immunity to the treatment. A relapse could occur, and this might be more difficult to deal with.

VACCINATIONS

There are a few extremely dangerous diseases that afflict cats, but fortunately there are vaccines that can dramatically reduce the risk of them infecting your Burmese. The bacteria and viruses that cause such diseases are often found in the air wherever there are cats. Discuss a program of immunization with your vet.

When a kitten is born, it inherits protection from disease via the colostrum of its mother's milk. Such protection may last for up to 16 weeks—but it varies from kitten to kitten and may last only six weeks. It is therefore recommended that your kitten be vaccinated against diseases at six to eight weeks of age just to be on the safe side. Boosters are required some weeks later and thereafter each year. Potential breeding females should be given boosters about three to four weeks prior to the due date. This will ensure that a high level of antibodies is passed to the kittens.

An important consideration with regard to the major killer diseases in cats is the treatment of infection. If a cat survives an infection, it will probably be a carrier of the disease and shed the pathogens continually throughout its life. The only safe course is therefore to ensure that your kittens are protected. The main diseases for which there are vaccinations are as follows:

Rabies: This is a disease of the neurological system. It is nonexistent in Great Britain, Ireland, Australia, New Zealand, Hawaii, certain oceanic islands, Holland, Sweden, and Norway. In these countries, extremely rigid quarantine laws are applied to ensure it stays that way. You cannot have your cat vaccinated against rabies if you live in one of these countries, unless you are about to emigrate with your cat. In all other countries, rabies vaccinations are either compulsory or strongly advised. They are given when the kitten is three or more months of age.

Feline panleukopenia: Also known as feline infectious enteritis, and feline distemper. This is a highly contagious viral disease. Vaccinations are given when the kitten is about eight weeks old, and a booster is given four weeks later. In high-risk areas, a third injection may be advised four weeks after the second one.

Feline respiratory disease complex: Often referred to as cat flu but this is incorrect. Although a number of diseases are within this group, two of them are especially dangerous. They are feline viral rhinotracheitis (FVR) and feline calicivirus (FCV). The vaccination for the prevention of these diseases is combined and given when the kitten is six or more weeks of age; a booster follows three to four weeks later.

Feline leukemia virus complex (FeLV): This disease was first recognized in 1964, and a vaccine became available in the US in about 1985. Like "cat flu," the name is misleading, because it is far more complex than a blood cancer, which is what its name implies. Essentially, it destroys the cat's immune system.

The disease is easily spread via the saliva of a cat as it licks other cats. It is also spread prenatally from an infected queen to her offspring via the blood, or when washing her kittens. This is why it is important to test all breeding cats for FeLV. Vaccination is worthwhile only on a kitten or cat that has tested negative. If a cat tests positive for the disease, it has a 70 percent chance of survival, though it will be a carrier in many instances.

Feline infectious peritonitis (FIP): This disease has various effects on the body's metabolism. There are no satisfactory tests for it, but intranasal liquid vaccinations via a dropper greatly reduce the potential for it to develop in the tissues of the nose.

PARASITES

Parasites are organisms that live on or in a host. They feed from it without providing any benefit in return. External parasites include fleas, lice, ticks, flies, and any other creature that bites the skin of the cat. Internal parasites include all pathogens, but the term is more commonly applied to worms in their various forms.

External parasites and their eggs can be seen with the naked eye. All can be eradicated with treatment from your vet. However, initial treatment will need to be followed by further treatments because most compounds are ineffective on the eggs. The repeat treatments kill the larvae as they hatch. It is also important that all bedding be treated or destroyed because this is often where parasites prefer to live when not on the host.

All cats are subject to a range of worm species. If worms multiply in the cat, they adversely affect its health. They will cause loss of appetite, wasting, and a steady deterioration in health. At a high level of infestation, they may be seen in the fecal matter, but normally it will require fecal microscopy by your vet. This will establish the species and the relative density of the eggs, thus the level of infestation.

Treatment is normally via tablets, but liquids are also available. Because worms are so common, the best husbandry technique is to routinely treat breeding cats for worms prior to their being bred, then for the queen and her kittens to be treated periodically. Discuss a testing and treatment program with your vet.

NEUTERING AND SPAYING

Desexing your cat is normally done when a female is about four months of age and somewhat later with a male. The operation is quite simple with a male but more complicated with a female. It is still a routine procedure. It is possible to delay estrus in a breeding queen, but the risk of negative side effects makes this a dubious course to take. Discuss it with your vet. A cat of any age can be neutered (male) or spayed (female); but if they are adults, they take some months (especially males) before they lose their old habits.

FIRST AID

Although you might think that such inquisitive creatures as cats would be prone to many physical injuries, this is not actually the case. They usually extricate themselves from dangerous situations because of their very fast reflexes. However, injuries do happen, and the most common is caused by the cat darting across a road and being hit by a vehicle. About 40 percent of cats die annually due to traffic accidents. The next level of injury will be caused by cats getting bitten or scratched when fighting among themselves, or being bitten by an insect, or by a sharp object getting lodged in their fur or feet.

If your cat is hit by a vehicle, the first thing to do is to try and place it on a board of some sort and remove it to a safe place. Do not lift its head because this might result in it swallowing blood into the lungs. Try to keep it calm by talking soothingly to it.

If the cat is still mobile, but has clearly been badly hurt, you must try and restrict its movements by wrapping it in a blanket or towel. If it is bleeding badly, try to contain the flow by wrapping a bandage around the body or leg to reduce the blood loss. With a minor cut, you should trim the hair away from the wound, bathe it, then apply an antiseptic or stem the flow with a styptic pencil or other coagulant.

If you suspect that your cat has been bitten by an insect and the result is a swelling, the poison is already in the skin so external ointments will have virtually no effect. The same is true of an abscess caused by fighting. The only answer is to let your vet use surgery to lance and treat the wound.

Fortunately, cats rarely swallow poison because they are such careful eaters. In all instances, immediately contact your vet and advise him of the kind of poison the cat has consumed.

If your cat should ever be badly frightened, for example, by a dog chasing and maybe biting it, the effect of this may not be apparent immediately. It may go into shock some time later. Keep the cat indoors so that you can see how it reacts. Should it go into shock and collapse, place a blanket around it and take it to the vet.

EXHIBITING BURMESE

From the first time cats were seriously exhibited in London in 1871, the cat show has been the very heart of the fancy. It is the place where breeders can have the merits of their stock assessed in a competitive framework, where all cat lovers can meet and discuss ideas, trends and needs, and where new products for cats can be promoted. It is the only event in which you have the opportunity of seeing just about every color and pattern variety that exists in the Burmese breed.

Even if you have no plans to become a breeder or exhibitor, you should visit at least one or two cat shows to see what a quality Burmese looks like.

TYPES OF SHOW

Shows range from the small informal affairs that attract a largely local entry to the major all-breed championships and specialty exhibitions that can be spread over two or more days (but only one in Britain). A specialty is a show restricted either by breed or by hair length (short or long). In the US, it is quite common for two or more shows to run concurrently at the same site.

SHOW CLASSES

The number of classes staged at a given show will obviously reflect its size, but the classes fall into various major divisions. These are championships for whole cats, premierships for altered cats, open classes for both of the previous cats, kittens, and household pets. In all but the pet class, there are separate classes for males and females. There are then classes for all of the color and pattern varieties. At a small show, the color/patterns may be grouped into fewer classes than at a major show.

All classes are judged against the standard for the breed, other than pet classes, in which the exhibits are judged on the basis of condition and general appeal, or uniqueness of pattern. An unregistered Burmese can be entered into a pet class, and it will be judged on the same basis as would a mixed breed. A kitten in the US is a cat of four months of age but under eight months on the day of a show. In Britain a kitten is a cat of three or more months and under nine months on the show day.

A show Burmese will require extra grooming, but even so, its short coat makes the job quick and easy.

AWARDS AND PRIZES

The major awards in cats are those of Champion and Grand Champion, Premier and Grand Premier. In Britain, a cat must win three challenge certificates under different judges to become a champion, while in the US it must win six winner's ribbons. In both instances, these awards are won via the open class. Once a cat is a champion, it then competes in the champions' class and becomes a grand based on points earned in defeating other champions. The prizes can range from certificates, ribbons and cups to trophies and cash.

Wins in kitten classes do not count toward champion status. Champion status in one association does not carry over to another, in which a cat would have to win its title again based on the rules of that association. The rules of competition are complex, and any would-be exhibitor should obtain a copy of them from their particular registry.

The general format of shows, while differing somewhat from one country to another, are much the same in broad terms. A Burmese will enter its color or pattern class. If it wins, it will progress to compete against other group winners in its breed, and ultimately compete for best of breed. If classes have been scheduled for all of the recognized colors and patterns in all of the recognized breeds, then a Best in Show will be the ultimate award. This is the dream of every cat exhibitor.

JUDGING

As stated earlier, cats are judged against their written standard rather than against each other. A winning cat is one that records the highest total of points, or, put another way, the least number of demerit marks. In the US cats are taken to the judge's table for assessment, but in Britain the judge moves around the pens with a trolley. In the US, judging is done in front of the public, but in the UK judging is normally done before the public is allowed into the hall. The exhibit owners are requested to leave the hall during judging.

CAT PENS

When you arrive at the cat show, a pen will be allocated to your cat. This is an all-wire cage. In Britain, the rules governing

Houseplants are a temptation to just about every cat. Play it safe by not keeping any poisonous ones in your home.

The Burmese is a totally distinctive cat that is not comparable to any other breed.

what can be placed into the cage are very rigid. This is because there can be no means of identifying the owner of the cat when the judge arrives at that pen. Thus, the blanket, the litter box and the water vessel must all be white. In the US the pens are highly decorated with silks, gorgeous cushions, and so on because the cat is taken to another pen for judging.

THE EXHIBITION BURMESE

Obviously, a Burmese show cat must be a very sound example of its breed. Its coat must be in truly beautiful condition because the level of competition is extremely high at the major events. At more local affairs, the quality will not be as high, which gives more exhibitors a chance to pick up victories in the absence of the top cats of the country. The male cat must have two descended testicles and have a valid vaccination certificate against feline enteritis that was issued at least seven days before the show. It should have tested negative for feline leukemia (and/or any other diseases as required by your registry).

A show cat must be well-mannered because if it should bite or claw the judge, it is hardly likely to win favor. It could even be disqualified, depending on the regulations of your registry. In any case, such a cat could not be examined properly by the judge, so this alone would preclude it from any hope of winning. It must therefore become accustomed to such treatment by being handled very often as a kitten by friends and relatives.

ENTERING A SHOW

You must apply to the show secretary for an entry blank and a schedule. The secretary will list the classes and state the rules of that association. The entry form must be completed and returned, with fees due, by the last date of entry as stipulated for that show. It is very important that you enter the correct classes; otherwise, your cat will be eliminated and your fee forfeited. If you are unsure about this aspect, you can seek the advice of an exhibitor of your acquaintance, or simply call the show secretary, who will advise you.

SHOW ITEMS

When attending a show you will need a variety of items. They include a cat carrier, litter box, blankets, food and water vessels, food, your cat's own supply of your local water if necessary, disinfectant, first aid kit, grooming tools, paper towels, entry pass, vaccination certificates, show catalog to check the entry for your cat and when it is likely to be judged, a small stool, and decorations for the pen. You may also wish to take your own food. Indeed, it would be wise to invest in a collapsible cart or trolley to transport all of the above!

The best advice is that you should visit shows and talk with exhibitors so that you can get the feel of things before you make the plunge yourself.

INDEX